Absence Notes

Absence Notes

Michael Woods

Templar Poetry

Published in 2011 by Templar Poetry
Templar Poetry in an imprint of Delamide & Bell

Fenelon House
Kingsbridge Terrace
58 Dale Road, Matlock, Derbyshire
DE4 3NB

www.templarpoetry.co.uk

ISBN 978-1-906285-31-9

Copyright © Michael Woods 2011

Michael Woods has asserted his moral right to be identified as the author
of this work in accordance
with the Copyright, Designs and Patents Act 1988

All rights reserved. This book is sold subject to the condition
that it shall not, by way of trade or otherwise, be lent, resold, hired out
or otherwise circulated without the publisher's prior consent, in any form
of binding or cover other than that in which it is published and without
a similar condition including this condition being imposed on
the subsequent purchaser

For permission to reprint or broadcast these poems write to
Templar Poetry

A CIP catalogue record of this book is available from the British Library

Typeset by Pliny
Graphics by Paloma Violet
Author photo by Phil Callow

Printed in India

For Dawn, my Northern light

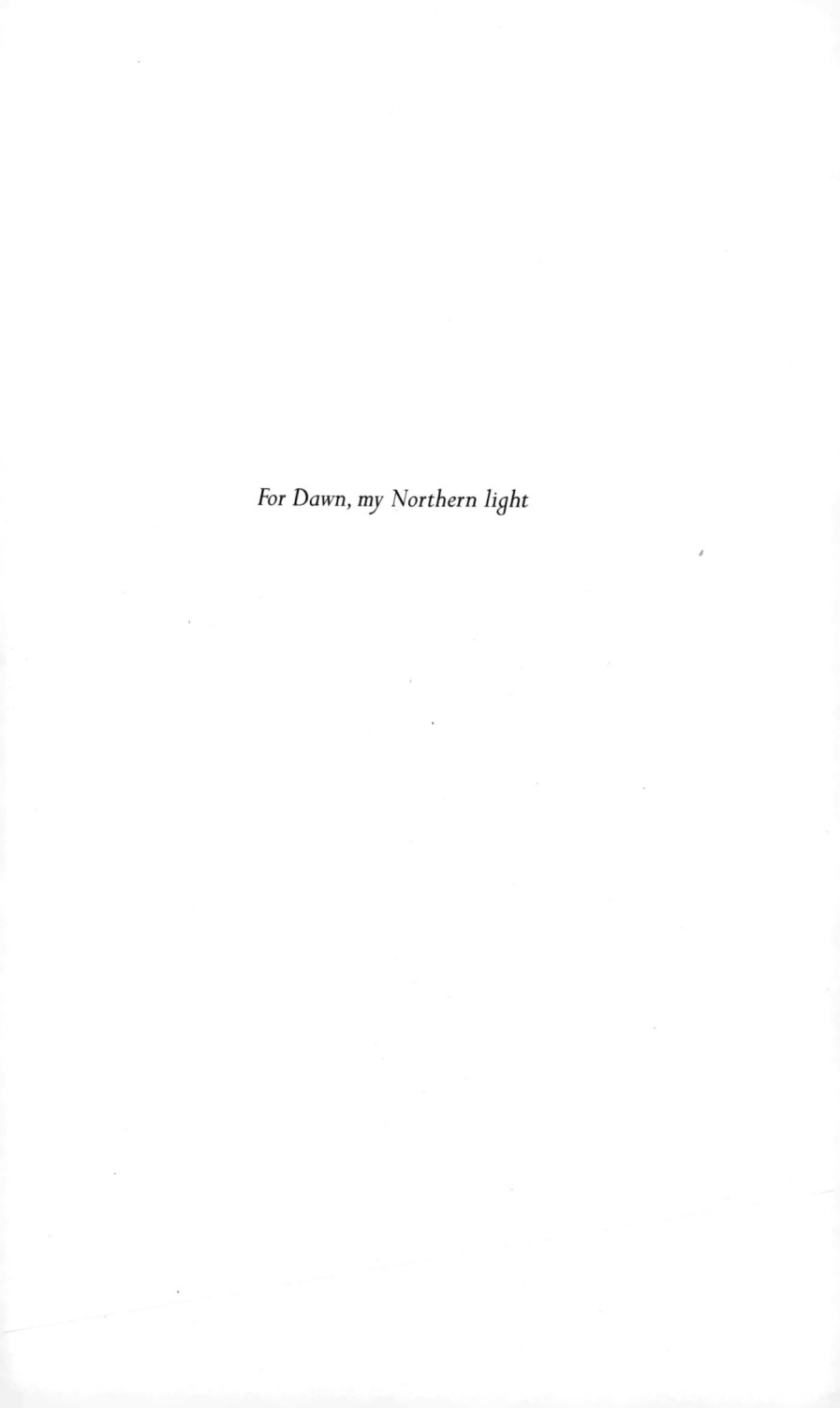

Acknowledgements

Joseph, 2nd Prize Three Choirs Competition, 1997; *To The Darts Players,* Highly Commended in the Stafford Poetry Competition 1998; *Nexus*, Poetry Competition Anthology 1998; *George*, Published in *Orbis; Frequencies,* Highly Commended in The Silver Wyvern Competition 2001, published in anthology; *Buil na mBlath*, Silver Wyvern, Poetry on the Lake Anthology 2001; *Dances, Gnossienne 1, Gnossienne 2, Gnossienne 3,* Silver Wyvern, anthology 2002; *Kevin de Medici,* Supplementary Prize in the Bridport Poetry Competition 2003, published in the Bridport Anthology; *Manden*, Highly Commended in The Silver Wyvern Competition 2003; *Barbecue*, 3rd Prize Ledbury Poetry Competition 2003; *Low Dividend*, published in *The Oxford Magazine* 2003; *Afterwards*, "Challenges" Anthology 2005 – Biscuit Publishing; *Kites,* Templar Poetry Anthology 2006; *The Prospect of Change*, Runner up in the Ragged Raven Poetry Competition, 2006 (Ragged Raven Anthology 2007); *Tandem*, published in Ragged Raven Anthology 2007; *Casting Off, Out of Fashion*, Faber (Ed. Carol Ann Duffy); *A Bluebell from St Beuno's, Answering Back*, Faber 2007 (Ed. Carol Ann Duffy); *The Value of Nothing*, Merit in Poetry Nottingham Competition 2007; *Leavings*, Virginia Warbey Competition Anthology 2007; *Footings,* Ver Poets Anthology 2007; *Callow End,* First Prize – Poetry Yearbook Competition 2007; *A Bluebell From St Beuno's, Templar* Poetry Anthology 2008; *Windhover Bovver,* Templar Poetry Anthology 2008.

Contents

I

Afterwards	3
Joseph	4
Footings	6
Kites	7
The Daisy Chain	8
Tandem	9
First Communion	10
Nexus	11
Shed	12
Marmalade	13
Great Uncle Graham	14
Jammy Dodgers	15
Low Dividend	16
Leavings	17
Ireland From the Gower	19

II

Occulis Mentabilis	23
Princess	24
Facula	25
Dublin	26
Sunflowers	27
The Wind Chimes	28
George	29
Becky	30
Last Impressions	32
All Change	34
To The Darts Players	35

The Value of Nothing	36
Kevin de Medici	38
Windhover Bovver	39
Casting Off	40
Clocher D'Enfer	41

III

The Prospect of Change	45
Semper Fidelis	46
Recipe	48
Photosynthesis	49
Béal na mBláth	50
A Bluebell From St Beuno's	52

IV

Dances	55

V

Manden	67
Sabrina	70
Barbecue	71
Sotto Voce	72
Absence Notes	73
Callow End	74

VI

Elected Silence	77

I

Afterwards

The Jungfrau wears the same clothing.
From the window her shoulders seem smooth.
Distance is always deceptive.
I could warm to her - but that's past.

The difficulty of her faces is replaced
by my difficulties in this room.
Its exactness hides no crevasses.
I'm only helped by the odd hand-hold
of a starched nurse, who I hear now,
thwacking a sheet for an empty bed.

The curtness of the sound calls all
the echo to mind of the day it happened.
The pitons lost their bite on the rock.

I swim back from the glacier,
make an attempt at my shoe-laces.

Joseph

I

It was all tension
in the delivery room,
and you still seemed
glimpsed galaxies away,
pouring your heart out
in the automatic writing
of the foetal monitor's pen
that traced its racing.

I heard each beat
as an outside broadcast
through a squeaky speaker
live-wired to your scalp.
These electric things made
more than a potential difference
as the nurse noticed your distress.
The machine plotted nothing
and found its origin.

Shocked into memory,
all I recalled was our first
virtual meeting in those
early scanning days when,
searched for like fish by sonar,
you showed up shadowy
in your secret space, waving a hand to me
that could be a plesiosaur's paddle,
a coelacanth's fin - semaphore from
an oceans away womb-home,
moon distant where you had landed.

Then, in the blink of an aeon,
you broke radio silence,
translating yourself again
into the language of graph lines.

II

I saw you born from water
into air as you barged
into the summer.
You were an astronaut to my eye,
space-walking from the mother ship
but blood-roped still,
already miming our every voyage.

It was the quick slow motion
of it all that lives in me -
you coming from your sea of tranquillity,
washed up by the amniotic tide;
that suspended second when you looked
and held me in the forever of your face,
before you drew breath,
before you cried.

Footings

Three years old -
you cast your expert eye
over the shallow footings
I have dug.

Your tongue concentrates
as you squat, squinting
along the tight twine line
we pegged to mark the path.

Looking for the level
I shovel sand and gravel,
trusting that brick,
block and stone,
stamped by your shoes,
will bear weight when
you count the days
as I do.

Kites

We flew our kite at Greatstone -
the usual diamond shape,
tail-weighted with a string
of bow-ties made from newspaper.

Airborne for hours -
our arms aching at the strain
of the struggling thing,
we'd lash it to the fence
and watch it fly.

My father would have us
send messages up the line:
paper squares, a hole ripped in the centre.

They swivelled like fishing spoons
into a new perspective,
fluttered to a world
unknown above our heads.

Today, I fly a kite with you
and watch you watch it dance.
I see it shrinking from my eye
as you leap in your delight,
and I pay out the line.

The Daisy Chain

for Lucy

Our garden's garland for your hair:
I thread for you a daisy chain -
this year, next year, sometime, never.

I register your knowing stare,
you've guessed I'll use the same refrain -
our garden's garland for your hair.

You babble through the meal we share,
your tea-time strawberries leave their stain;
this year, next year, sometime, never.

The wings of bees unzip the air,
your infant's fingers feel again
our garden's garland for your hair.

The kiss of sunlight kills despair,
I let the summer take the strain;
this year, next year, sometime, never.

I utter now my silent prayer,
believing words make live again
our garden's garland for your hair -
this year, next year, sometime, never.

Tandem

Today, you belted around the racecourse,
your knees pumping up and down, propelling
for the first time, without stabilisers,
you and your fixed wheeled, fire chief bike. Yelling

useless injunctions about the need to brake,
I knew that you were only bent on speed -
flashing down a corridor of trees, freed
to fight flames, with both our lives at stake.

Pedals from the past generate their voltage…
my yellow *Triang* clanks a crank against
the chain guard. Five, and fretful for my age,
I'm worried it will chip the shiny paint.

But your joy's like a boy's who's just learned to ride,
unalloyed, like your callipers' blue steel.
I am your proxy but for you it's real.
My legs race for you. It comes back like the tide…

no fancy gears, just turning of the years
that brings us all within each other's spheres.
You light the night, powered by your dynamo.
I feel our fathers' hands, at last, let go.

First Communion

Saint Mary's, Rockingham Road.
You might expect miracles and fine bone china
from an address like that and be forgiven.
But here was peeling paint and rotting gates,
a half-mile trek to lunch each day
and the reek of runny cabbage.

Sashed and veiled, the boys and girls
wore godly clothes like grooms and brides,
benched in rows and trying to be good
not eating sudden jelly on top of undigested god.

The parish priest was welcomed
to our breakfast in the winning way
of little children - coaxing the flat battery
of his name up the gradient of decorum:
Good morning Canon Geor-eor-eor-eorge -
with just enough affection to let him know
he needn't give up the ghost just yet.

I watched his sweating head, the dome of which
shone with the same hairless sheen as the shell
of my egg, just lifted from the pan; was struck
by its resemblance to the head- or the head's to it.
I hoped for a runny yolk, was out of luck, I think.
Whatever the case, I took my guilty spoon,
bashed in the top – sliced and sliced again,
worried that my bread was bursting through his brain.

Nexus

Tended year on year it became
their apple tree - his favourite,
growing between the hawthorn hedge
and potato drills where love
rooted itself in the garden.

Each Spring greened new wood;
Each Summer sunned fresh fruit.
Autumn apples hung heavy but grew,
juice-freighted, beyond her reach.
She watched them fall through Winter.

And so, the tree was busy
making a reflection of itself
beneath the frigid earth,
its taproot drinking the ground dry .

Shed

Some were presents from Michael Lannigan:
the bits that never lost their temper, planes
that belonged to Jack, whose embossed name
is as clear as when his working days began.
The shed has let him leave the world behind
and gives him time to sing along to tapes
of tenors that he loves. His teaspoon scrapes
the mug he stirs and stirs just to unwind.
The saws he sets have yet to lose their teeth,
and plane blades, like the chisels, keep their edge.
Gauged, honed on oil anointed stone, tools shed
a 3 in 1 reminder of belief.

The right tools make a job a piece of cake,
I hear him say. *Looked after, they won't break*.
Man's solace is this sunned and shadowed space,
where everything is in and out of place.

Marmalade

As my grandfather lay dying in his bed
my grandmother perched on its edge
munching toast and marmalade (rough cut).

I marvel at this now - to conserve the memory
as much as anything, I suppose.
But to think his last repose

was met first with the false-toothed
mastication of a wife
eating toast at his toes

is a bit hard to swallow.

Great Uncle Graham

Uncle Graham's famous in our family
for performing feats of fretwork in bed,
while his long-suffering wife lay beside him,
enduring the sawdust and insanity.

He'd saw away for hours at a stretch,
only stopping to piss in a beer bottle,
then set to again, sawing and shaping;
but Gertie was all he ever finished.

She went gaga long before her time,
locked inside the prison of her head,
while her gaoler brought new work to bed.
Their daughters, shamming sleep, were scared to death.

He'd fling their baby dolls into the fire;
hair would hiss in the grate, wax faces melt.
As his eyes blazed in dazed dementia,
both girls wondered who'd be next.

Jammy Dodgers

Biting into a *Jammy Dodger*
reminds me of Roger whose father
set out to sail around the world.
Mocking at first, then marvelling,
our class traced his racing route around
the globe with a measle rash of map pins,
learning about logs, leagues and nautical miles.

Late at night we listened to the shipping forecast,
place names recited like a litany at mass -
deadpan as boys' voices picking football teams by lot
but doomed at last to choose the boy who couldn't pass.

Stone, scissors paper; scissors, paper, stone.
Rockall, Malin Head, Dogger, Fisher, Tyne.

Search for Lone Sailor Called Off.
Trimeran, *Teignmouth Electron* Found
Abandoned Off The Azores.

Children flocked like gulls after a ferry's easy pickings
when Roger bought their time with boxes
of *Jammy Dodgers*, biscuits with a bleeding
heart. They'd stay and play with him at break
until the bell told them to leave him grieving
in the grey, deserted ocean-of-a-yard
for his dead and undiscovered dad.

Low Dividend

It was just as I was beating
up the Yorkshire puddings,
and three weeks before I was rewired.

Back from the betting shop,
he told me we had the pools up.
Twenty-three points. New carpet.
Dresses for the bairns.

Cortisone injections. Pigeons.
They kept his mind off things
at first.

But he went -
with a hard winter,
and the smell of dinner
in the back kitchen.

Leavings

October, one of the rosary months,
seems more like May or June as we work
for the last time in the garden, counting
decades bathed for now in glorious light.

We have unearthed the past. It waits
wrapped in nostalgic polythene, transformed
into the real presence of lavender,
rhododendron and Japanese nutmeg.

Like vital transplant organs kept on ice
they offer something of the old life to the new.
The removal van will come for them
on Monday. We rake through leaves in mourning.

My father straps a rope around a trunk
he made one drizzling Ruislip afternoon,
the one in which we used to keep our toys.
Full of oddments now, he tightly ties the lid.

Within the knowing walls we drink champagne,
wondering at celebration; the bubbles rise
like questions, thawed moments released
from the memory's melting berg.

Our last meal together in this house…
I urge my father to say the final grace
my mother has to finish. Afterwards,
we watch the progress of a tired sun.

The rooms are bare like Easter altars.
Shelves, stripped of books, are lost for words.

We talk of Yeats but can't look up the lines
that are forgotten. The walls seem to loosen.

My camera's shutter flinches in each room,
records in flashing fractions of a second
the composition of a home developed
in the dishes of slow days.

Our last goodbyes are frantic from the car.
You drive, and soon we reach the open road.
Searching stars for consolation I see
the pocked face of a mocking moon,
feel the years' elastic pull.

Ireland from the Gower

Walking the beach, we waded,
talked and waited for evening.
Wrack cracked beneath our feet,
strings of connected emerald spaces
like opalescent rosaries. Most mysteries,
I've since found, turn out to be sorrowful.

After dinner, talk and more talk in the bar.
Later, we listened to *Clannad* in the car,
drinking wine to the song of an Irish siren.
Common sense told us that blood was enough
to make us feel wrecked on the rock of our past.

As we looked to Ireland over the black bonnet
of your car, the tide was turning.

We met again a few weeks later.

Though a gulf was streaming
through your daggered days
and wintering your smiles,
something, like the undertow,
began to draw you to its hope
and warmed you for a while.

II

Occulis Mentabilis

Have a good time tonight. I might as well have said
I enjoy sprinkling arsenic on my bread.
I see your eyes across a candled table,
blue pools enchanting someone else's

come up specially for the occasion.
What wine warmed words will you murmur
when the night begins to sigh
and the moon moans for love?

Princess

I invent a world of ours
away from this.
A sarong would wrap you,
spun out of samite, light
as a breath from the blue.
I'd love you by a sapphire sea,
and you could be Sappho,
composing an ode to me.

Now, the West is where
your pleasure lies. Sibilant breeze
breathes into evening trees.
Sibylline language of leaves
spells the sound of your name,
a light sigh in suspiring night.

Facula

Outside, on the racecourse,
I can hear heat being
burned into the belly
of a hot air balloon.

Fire-sired, it swells to float
like an ovum in the air,
swallowing naked flame
into a cavernous crimson heart -
a hollow fleshing itself to straining fullness,
pulling on the rope umbilicus.

In a heaving second of release
the whole thing is airborne -
a fire-gorged fruit,
exotic, red and purple
against a ruddy gash
slashed across the Summer sky.

Buoyed above by heat,
it rises through the evening's
carnal, crimson light.
I am caught aware;
this self -sustaining flight
is a journey of longing
swept on the thermals
of approaching night,
spilling fire, light
and profligate heat
like a shimmering sunspot
flying forever.

Dublin

This pint of stout, though quietly settling
at the bar, is noticeably turbulent.
Gradually, its struggle with itself
resolves into a black body and white head.

Your gin and tonic mixes easily
but the drink is rather strong, you say.
We sit apart in sinking leather chairs.
Our tepid talk turns up a past we share.

The fair one from the dark pool; you surfaced
like a Liffey salmon, lithe and lovely -
breaking the silver meniscus of the night,
blanched with holy lunar light.

In the front seat of the car your shoulders
gleam like elvers lit by lamps in night-poached rivers.
Light slants across a road that reaches back
to wished for tomorrows as the Cherwell churns, churns.

Arching into the depths of the river,
diving into the pool of night,
a tail flicks, a flank flashes silver
in the moon-washed gloam, and is gone.

Sunflowers

They hang - burnt out,
shadows on a field of umber,
as autumn undresses the land.

Driving past, I tell myself
they're sowing next year's sun,
bleeding seed into the ground.

Not so many weeks ago,
sun-sent flower shadows slid
over the bonnet like polish.

Then, all earth seemed heated.
The sunflowers flamed,
you smouldered, and I burned.

Now, evening over,
leaving late for home,
I turn right onto the bypass.

Second gear through silent, silver light;
I'm driving past the sunflower field,
where summer's heat is buried.

I accelerate into the past,
as the moon spills itself
into the still pool of night.

The Wind Chimes

Aeolus is back.
You gave him his voice -
remember?

September sun's late
light slants towards alembic night,
raising a lazy breeze.

Aluminium tubes
work in concert, hung
in a suspense of air.

Compression and
rarefaction is all sound is
but what moves here

in the whorl of the ear
is the worked alchemy
of transmuting fire.

What golden echo
might be spared again,
heard through night's chasm?

George

I went to his cremation,
remembered his nervous body,
met his three fathers
and three mothers
who had pinballed him
from house to house.

George from bondage
had delivered George
with a nylon rope
bought from a garage.
He slung it, hung from the neck.
The proprietor didn't know
that it would tow him somewhere else.

He had been discovered in his tree
by a dog and its woman.
The words had stopped in his throat.
His tongue was a bung,
swollen and blue in his face.
He swung like a clapper in a bell
but told nothing.

Becky

I drove to meet you.
Wet slammed against the windscreen.
The glass misted, cleared and misted.
Wipers' rubbers could not sweep away
runnels of water that ran in tracks,
ceaseless through hours and days of rain;
droplets beaded the bonnet like a rosary.

I could risk it,
say there was emotion
in the skies that day;
anyway, the stretched pathos
of your body was no fallacy.

An afternoon in June
but the only bloom
was on your pallid face.
Dressed, as though expecting guests,
your alabaster fingers capped
with amethyst slivers of nails,
your lips livid with the ghastly paint
of posthumous art -
you waited.

An undertaker breezed me to your coffin.
The purple of your shroud,
a draped cape, appalled.
He swept it aside like a conjuror:
There she is!
But I knew there was no trick in this.
Nothing could bring you back now.

Hardly dressed against the rain,
I turned to leave the terrible vortex
of that room, staggered
into the gaping yawn of the afternoon,
the indelible print of your face
left like a watermark.

Last Impressions

You Norman Wisdomed in my living room,
Frank Spencered in my hall,
shared my meal, your nerves strung tighter
than my guitar, which you strummed to kill time.

Audition night for *Hobson's Choice* -
your chance to be a star on local radio.
I watched and listened, a replacement parent
peering through the studio's oblong panes.

I still have Radio Wyvern's letter
saying you'd been unsuccessful.
I came across it weeks after your young suicide.

You were once at *The Town's Talk*,
riding high on a wave of applause
but bowed out before it broke.

The facts speak for themselves.
You had been homed too often
to know what home was like.
Your 'dad' had dumped you
from his Ford Capri so often,
left you alone on pavements,
the victim of misjudgement,
you'd forgotten who you were.

There was snow on the ground
the day they burned you and the sky
hung heavy, threatening more.
Monochrome outside merged
with monotone inside
as the vicar did his best.

It was a theatrical exit. My eyes
glutted on that ghastly, sinking slab,
the synthetic symbolism
of earth taking you back.

Afterwards, in the numb car park,
your friends were crying,
their sobs muffled by the snow.

Climbing into the Beetle, I glanced in the mirror.
A stainless steel chimney caught my eye
and, above it, a shimmer in the sky.

All Change

The train is swallowing track.
Gravel ponds patch the way.
Another train passes us, on the way back.
Its windows are a reel of film played
like flak in fast, individual frames.
A mobile plays *Nokia* arpeggios.

The woman opposite has crocodile shoes.
She takes her 'phone to the toilet.
On her return she rhythmically strokes
a cup of *Kenco* hot chocolate whilst
reading *The Child in Time*.

Relax, says the carrier bag
discarded on the table between us.
Raindrops swarm like sperm
across the windows that flash
double-glazed destinies
and diode-lit promises of stations:
Paddington via Moreton-in-Marsh
and everywhere from Worcester.

Anonymous laptop log-ons
converge for a while in this
First Great Western carriage.
Orange minutes and Vodafone
Talktime 200 satellite in space
long before the tracks meet at infinity.
Swapped urban myths about false
mobile 'phones, skinned alive pets
and stolen kidneys are left
as unfinished as crosswords.

To the Darts Players

I marvel at the sight of all this flesh
fitting flights to plastic shafts with sausage
fingers. Then, balanced on the oche, mesh
mind and body in a beery marriage

that somehow amounts to concentration
strong enough to make the precise launch
of darts seem a graceful contemplation
upon motion made by men with a paunch.

The Value of Nothing

A time and motion man,
Bertram Walkwell kept
a padlocked cupboard
in his bedroom. Here he
hoarded every special offer
item held in any of
six local supermarkets.

Safely guarded by a shiny
Squire, packs of snacks,
soup and *Oxo* cubes
(all bargain buys) bulged
behind the bridging unit.

Come the weekend he'd be doodling
over sums he loved to do.

In the flat-pack kitchen
he'd weigh out weekly spuds
and sell them at a profit
to his wife, who waited
in a one woman queue,
clutching her brass clasped purse
while he eyed her over
half-moon specs,
rimlessly reflecting
bargain sixty-watters.

She'd cursed at first
but soon got used to his
penny pinching game,
as eyes do to the dark.

At night, he dreamed his
everlasting discount dream
in which she begged him
to play the percentage game,
and impossible numbers
of Tiger Tokens were redeemed
for love, or tumblers from Taiwan.

Kevin di Medici

Uncle Lorenzo really pisses me off.
The Magnificent, they call him.
He owns almost all of Florence.
Cosimo, my dad, says he'll get his hands on the lot one day.
He's always at the office; that's not my scene.

I hang out with a happening crowd.
We meet under David's dick,
sometimes drive out to Fiesole and frighten nuns.
Orsino, the arsehole, says it could become a habit.
I told him, said I couldn't see a future for me in banking.
Yes, we're loaded but the medici.co.it
bubble has to burst sometime.

Dad tarts about with poofs like Micky Angelo,
got him to paint my bedroom ceiling last year.
Mum had a makeover for the lounge thrown in.

I've got a bit of a racket going with the gold
traders on the Ponte Veccio. The butchers
don't like it but I'm first violin around here.

I've enrolled for a GNVQ in Leisure and Tourism.
I'm far sighted, see. Scrapping between nation states is crap,
has to stop sometime.
All that shit between Guelphs and Ghibellines
lost us Dante. Absolute pants, eh?

I've asked Mick to knock out some cardboard cut-outs
of D and B to flog on the bridge. If they go well, the next caper
will be T-shirts. Next? Well, I'm working with a mate
from Venice. Glarse souvenirs bust easy. I can't wait.

Windhover Bovver

Gerard Manley Hopkins Writes to R.B in Cockney Slang

Cream-crackered after me mornin' prayers,
out the window I clocked this 'awk - a bird
climbin' the apples 'n' pears o' the air.
Gor blimey! Would you Adam 'n' Eve it?
I'm searchin' me gravy train for a word
to celebrate the little sod's achieve
ment - when it buggered off! I was in stress,
lookin' f'me bird book - but no success.
Then I remembered. Old Felix Randal
borrowed it just before 'e popped 'is clogs…
No one else I've met could 'old a candle
to 'im. This country's goin' to the dogs.
Yours, *Gezza*. P.S. This Easter bonnet
should buckle under what the ac's write on it.

Casting Off

The Skerries flinch in the storm
as their rock piles are ramped by the sea.
I knit to the tune of the clock as I rock
through the rock-black, night after night.

The wool I pull from the tangle
of balls in the leather bag lived once,
lagged the legs and hot-tank bodies
of sheep that sleep without dreams.

Shorn, their warmth will froth again
but, like me, they were born to be worn –
our lives twisted together in skeins
that I turn into clothes for the town.

The needles are number eights.
I double knit the three-ply night
into stitches and rows. I know
the patterns as well as the knots

that were veins on the backs of his hands
or the black of the space where his face
used to be, or the giveaway diamond
design of the cable-knit, double-knit

sweater, the one that I sweated myself
from the scores of the pores in my sin
when time before time I'd wish
that the sea would wash him away.

Clocher D'Enfer

Sunday swallows spitfire-strafed the church tower,
then sang on staves of wires, conducting notes
that were themselves through clear full-throttle throats,
suggesting they had knowledge of their power
of flight to thrill. We watched them for an hour
or so before you let on what devotes
you to *grandpère* - led us through golden fields of oats
to *clocher d'enfer*. In this clearing, even the sun lours.

You said more: British airmen were hanged there,
like sallies for a carillon of bells.
Some were untold. He hid them beneath bare
boards in his *blanchisserie*. So, *Courmelles*,
traduced, made heaven out of hell. *Mon frère*,
I hear swallows, you see *hirondelles*.

III

The Prospect of Change

The beggar in the car park after mass
is well versed in the habits of the faithful.
Some cannot forgive him his trespasses
against their wallets, however needful
he may be. But this man begs with style.
Like an extra from a parable he smiles
as if he doesn't take but rather gives
the means by which the giver lives.

From tramp to gent he transubstantiates
himself. His language of urbanity
converts a cadge to existential quiz
when uttered with the polished charm that's his,
by archly asking anyone in range
of his fluence: *Any prospect of change?*

Semper Fidelis

Worcester, backing Royal claims
restored Charles to the throne,
it now keeps faith with retail chains,
the shops are mostly clones.

Next is next to *River Island*,
Past Times vies for room,
a poster pants near the hot dog stand,
'Ann Summers Coming Soon!'

The cheapo bookshop's closing down
and 'everything must go',
it will open in another town
where business rent is low.

Edward Elgar cast in bronze
has a pigeon guano head.
The Severn's fighting, lead-free swans
beak meals of tourists' bread.

Blackfriars car park blights the sky,
built on a planner's nod;
the ghosts of monks must wonder why
it's more in vogue than God.

Glory to God in the High Street,
the tills ring out their joy
as Christmas bars become replete
with money saved for toys.

A club spills onto Angel Place,
its stomach shouts, *Kebabs*!
Lit by a well-used moon's pocked face,
police vans wait like cabs.

Greggs and *Smiths* feed gut and eye
but hardship's not a liar -
Big Issue's written in the sky
as a busker juggles fire.

Recipe

Invaginate an eel before it can
escape to the heaving Sargasso;
scorify all the gold you can find in
an alembic stolen from Paracelsus
for the express purpose of causing chaos.
Transmute all air to invar;
burn the pre-Socratic monists
in an athanor for three millennia
until one lets you into his secret,
and the Logos renovates all words
to their prelapsarian power.
Make a cake with mud and a flayed beaver
so as to challenge the very word *cake*.
Quote Robert Frost, paraphrase Stevens:
the better made it is the better -
the more equal to life it will be and
the less life will matter for that matter.
As you eviscerate a live white chicken
in a red wheelbarrow, let the listening
be fresh and the looking nothing less.

Photosynthesis

Eight minutes is all it takes for light
to reach us from the sun. Afternoon
rays are sugaring the fruiting plum tree
in our knowing garden. A synergy
of water, air and chlorophyll will soon
have branches bending under bursting freight.
Next week, there will be bird-stoned yeasting piles,
catalysed from over ninety million miles.

I don't know what this tree holds out against us
but every year it drops some plums next door.
These are gathered by our giving neighbour
who turns the fruit to sickly wine by Christmas.
It seems a shame that light came all this way
to connive with them, and poison such a day.

Béal na mBláth

(The Mouth of Flowers)

This orchid is known
as *Dracula's Bucket*.
It lures iridescent bees
to almost certain death.
The camera shows
us every intimacy:
anther, stamen, ovary.

Its honeyed parts drip nectar
into the waiting well of itself.
A bee craving the inside
of the juice-cave drowns
in extreme close-up.

A hungry pollinator
escapes only if acting
as aerial proxy in sex
between two blooms,
signs its own death warrant
if it comes too close
to the mouth of flowers.

One worker survives
all sorties it seems -
pollen on its head,
tongue and abdomen -
soaked in a syrup
he could live on for days.

But here is a flower
open like the lips of a lover.

He enters the darkness -
falls through the slit
as a boy through
a bloom-covered
trapdoor in time.

Not the open mouth
of a succubus coming
for his seed in the night
or the slow-dropping peace of sleep
but the barrel of a vampiric gun
ready to bleed the life out of him.

A Bluebell from St. Beuno's

Weary after a long term we drove to Wales -
his world for a while where *springs not fail*.
After the study session at the *Bod Eryn* Hotel
we tucked into pied beauty for lunch -
trout and almonds, chips with a twist of lemon.
We traced our way over his pastoral forehead,
the turrets of St. Beuno's set square
against the Vale of Clwyd.

Not the right thing to do, perhaps
but I picked a flower that went to press.
What he might have said to me about
my act of stealth as I slipped the bluebell
between the passions of his poems
I know I'll never know but, since then,
veins have been visibly bound, fastened
to a page that's almost the colour of flesh.

IV

Dances

To what serves mortal beauty — | dangerous; does set danc- /
                                                       Ing blood

(Gerard Manley Hopkins)

Gymnopédie I

Here you are inside
the room of nakedness,
this stanza a place to
pace out the length
and breadth of truth.

Your life is the gymnasium,
the exercise of bodies;
and so you move,
stunning me to stone.

I know you could name
with ease every muscle,
tendon, blood vessel;
anatomise me - please.

Gymnopédie II

Stone imitates skin
in the marble of statues
worked on to make
bodies like stone.

Chiselled muscle
is smoothly hard
to the touch of newly
loved hands.

This can't be dressed
with words.
Strip them to leave
only the bared wire
of truth that, grasped,
reminds you you're alive.

Gymnopédie III

There is you;
there is space,
sound, silence.

Your body's
perfect pitch
is tuned

to the music
of slow time,
preparing

for movement,
real presence,
pure line.

Sarabande I

You exercise alone.
T'ai Chi, you say
and I'm seeing
in slow motion -
your room
your space
your body
and a low, slow sun
grazing the ridge
of the chameleon hills,
rose-flamed now
like a volcano's mouth
above the cauldron night.

Sarabande II

We practise, practise, practise
our karate- kihon, kata, kumite:
There is dance and danger
in this empty-handed art.
It's difficult but we keep

close distance in this
ballet of violence,
work on tai sabaki:
body evasion.

Sarabande III

Satie in Honfleur
wrote letters to himself.
He composed, he said,
naked piano music:
gymnopédies,
sarabandes,
gnossiennes.

The truth is simple
and we're dancing it;
don't stop, don't stop
the dance.

Gnossienne I

Gankaku:
a crane standing
on a rock.

You learned the kata
knowing stillness
counts as much
as movement.

You stand,
ideogram of flesh,
one-legged
on your rock,

an appoggiatura
made visible,
alive to the moment.

Gnossienne II

Perfection of form
comes from perfection
of knowledge, gnosis.

So, this kata
is the crane of Knossos,
proof against the minotaur.

Each block, punch
and kick thwarts
whatever threatens,

threads a way through
a labyrinth felt
by unbound feet.

You stand, perfect
in balance, gankaku,
the poem you dance.

Gnossienne III

A Giverny of colour
refracted through stained glass
daubs the floor we walk on.
The blurred focus of dreamed
distance in fields of red and green
floods through where I've seen
you a thousand times
turning through light
that dances in your hair.

V

Manden

The moon is *in elevatio* but I hear
the ice-boom *fractio* from the fjord,
your echoing words, your words -
I'm leaving you, Torvald toll
like the curse of a troll in my head.

Snow sheets split on the roof
and slide through thawing days.
I listen at the jamb of the door,
stuck between the past and future,
to the stopped clock of my heart.

Oscar can't come to terms with your going.
He is vacant at school with a mind
on his mother, not lessons. My lessons,
like his are loathsome to learn. He's hidden
the trumpet you bought him.

Ivar thinks you're on holiday.
His sword is his favourite toy
and drives Anne-Marie crazy
with his 'practice' day after day.
He's planning a homecoming display.

Emmy says there's a troll in the fjord
that took you away. She plays with her dolls
Calling, *Mummy, Mummy, Mummy*.
She started to injure herself. First it was the dolls.
Then she took blame on herself for the hole in our house.

She rocks in her bed in the night.
I tried to keep it from them for weeks
but, as you know, truth hates to hide.
It is a stone in my head that breaks
the ice on the stagnant pond of the past.

I couldn't bear to give away your clothes.
I had a mind to post everything you have
and everything you gave before your move
back across the miles you put between us
but the smell of you was on them so they stayed.

I thought last Christmas was the worst
that could be lived. But what about the next?
I toyed with the baubles from the tree,
saw myself more distorted the closer
I got to my reflection, doubled in dread, my two

selves split between light and shadow.
One of them fell from the tree, shattered on the parquet,
glittering splinters among the needled green. I looked
at our lives in those facets and shivered at scattered
compounds of eyes, our living lies.

I've visited Rank's grave quite often,
left flowers for you. April is with us already.
The soil's softened and sun heats the days.
Blossom is bursting through snow in the thaw
but I don't trust the Spring any more.

Meaningless snowdrops are blooming. I know
I've been blind, wrong. Instead of the song
of the birds, all I hear again and again
is the sound of a door slamming shut,
cringing hinges, hurt air in the hall

reverberating, rippling out into
the silent years that lie waiting and dead.
I'm locked in the hell of a cell that's my head,
that last waft from your cloak as you left
leaving the trace of your scent behind.

Icebergs shoulder each other in the thaw.
The glacier growls and ice sheets split.
The fjord frowns its crenellations of firs
on the skiers who've finished their season
and I see you still - cloaked and determined,

steaming unstoppably back to the place
of your birth, iron to the earth, drawn home
like a struck rod magnetised, knowing your place,
able to find True North. I sense your needle move
and I wait, Nora. I wait in the wings of your love.

Sabrina

> *...she revived*
> *And underwent a quick immortal change,*
> *Made goddess of the river. (Milton - Comus)*

I flow here still, the dark depths of me
nymph-helped and strong against
these river men who ply their trade
across my flanks. From bank to bank
they ferry the public, are paid in pence.

The oars are waved like wands
by one of them who says he finds it hard
to master my current as I take even the swans
further than they'd dreamt of going.
My water carries weight, I know.
From somewhere I hear another voice;
it's muffled but I can just make out the words:
Be wise, and taste. My surface ripples.
I jumped, once, into what is now myself,
my mortal past drowned by kind Nereus.

So, now I'm a river goddess
on a May bank holiday.
Suddenly lost in love, I trust
a man who says *the river's pushing down.*
I want him to drink my wetness dry.

In this falling dark I feel the keel of his boat
as he pulls, pulls against me, struggling
in the wake of *The Pride of the Midlands* -
blazing its lights towards Stourport.
I want him for nocturnal sport.

Barbecue

It seems innocent enough but this word
can turn the whole of anything that's cooked
on coals to shit, a marinated turd
or Chernobyl melt-down; something that, looked
at closely, could just as easily pass
for some poor creature's head or heart or arse.
Smoke from 'beard' and 'bum': every garden's stench
smells so much worse translated from the French.

Then there's its abbreviation - *Barbie* -
outdoor party invitation to skewer,
then burn, a leggy blonde in effigy
so that even Ken won't recognise her.
And what will he remember as her thighs
drip into the pyre? Lies. Her lethal lies.

Sotto Voice

The way the marble's marked
gives away the rhythm of his chisel
as he worked and worked to set me free.

His hands chased my brain, veins –
honed my hands, thighs, limbs, loins
to a perfection of stillness.

Because he turned to stone I move now
through the fluence of his telling touch.
I am his speaking, sighing own.

Petrified, I breathe his gone life.
Listen. Holy stones can move men's hearts
whose hearts are wholly stone.

Absence Notes

Photographs are the certificates of presence (Derrida)

This solstice moon is a host held high
by a priest of the invisible. Monstrance
night, prophet of loss, develops distance
from the sun like a negative. A cry
caves that unkissed mouth, desolate
as Masaccio's Eve. Her eyes are on
time's arrow and the event horizon's
gulf where weightless men play golf, tessellate
a photographed mosaic of her dark side
to map a mystery only Sappho knew.
Apollo shoots his shots in silver thousands,
lays bare her ways, shows how she pulls the tide.
She knows. From here the earth is out of view
as waves wash Friday's footprints from the sand.

Callow End

Cows, mist-drowned, merge with sheep
in this soft focus Malverns morning.
Powick church has shivered out of night.
The sun is a white-hot coin struck
in the mint of the sky, unquenchable
and incensed by vapour from the fields.
Nothing is not what it seems as the river floods
and water strains to wed itself to land.
The horizon shimmers like the inside of a forge
or quivering air around the after burner
of the low flying jet that sometimes scuds the hills.

Taking the bend, I see the village announce itself
in what seems to be a claim to wisdom;
the sign is bald - blocks of black on white.
But this isn't Italy. It doesn't warn with a red slash
that its limits have been reached. So, I sweep
beyond its parish pale, apparently boundless
but sensing the car break some meniscus
as it passes deep magnetic fields.

In this winter's wet and ice it's odd to think
the hedges hangar what will fledge and fly.
So, I signal, put my foot down and roll the car
over the camber to avoid the wash of what might
overtake me. A rear-view glance is all it takes
to show the whole reflected shrinking scene -
less substance than accident, and the open road ahead.

VI

Elected Silence

Whereof we cannot speak...

The devil's anvil's quilted here
where words are processed for the ear
and, just like phones' predictive text,
the eye can see what's coming next.

Wedged between the church and state
Westminster's kettled students wait,
the latest enemy within
behind the miners, claiming kin.

A media managed garden tryst
is swallowed now in winter's mist.
Sick roses incubate their worms
and these rough beasts could go full term.

Here are the architects of choice
but deaf to challenge, any voice
that shows it knows rebut, refute
are different things, and won't play mute.

Words stuck fast like frozen points
thaw slower than arthritic joints
or memory of summer's shocks
while promises lie on the rocks.

Own the words and own the mind,
speak in Braille to dupe the blind.
The loom of language here unspools,
reinventing grammar's rules,

writing off as crass, pedantic
anyone who says semantics
matter when it comes to teasing
meaning from what some call *queasing*.

Word and meaning's quick divorce
lets bankers redefine remorse
as something with a use-by date
and 'clear' now means to obfuscate.

They'll pay for science, not for art;
Now Albion's cold, sclerotic heart
beats in place of Blake's before
where bankers take, don't ask, for more.

Broad Street, Bread Street: Blake and Donne,
Milton the Republican
addressed themselves to angels, God;
their poetic feet well shod

with mettle and the need to tell
what turns a heaven into hell.
Factions' fractious tolling knells
the sound of a division bell.

Not a mile North-East of here
In Finsbury, Bunhill's vault uprears;
the bones of William Blake at rest
rise up again for the oppressed.

His shade weeps for what might have been,
His Lamb and Tyger scan the scene:
The razing of Jerusalem,
Playing out in front of them.

Elected silence he knows well
is empty as a blown egg's shell.
Was England's house for sale? In bold -
a sign outside the door reads: SOLD